The Primary Art Handbook

Written and Illustrated by:

Lindsey Apps
Karen Baxendale Manning
Adrienne Dawes
Dianne Williams

Published by
Topical Resources

The Primary Art Handbook is available from all good Educational Bookshops and by mail order from:

Topical Resources
P.O. Box 329
Broughton
Preston
Lancashire
PR3 5LT

Topical Resources publishes a range of Educational Materials for use in Primary Schools and Pre-School Nurseries and Playgroups.

FOR LATEST CATALOGUE Tel/Fax 01772 863158

All materials needed for the activities in this book can be obtained from:

PISCES
Papers and Art Material Contractors
Westwood Studios
West Avenue
Crewe
CW1 3AD
Tel: 01270 216211
Fax: 01270 586150

Copyright © Topical Resources

First Published September 1997

Printed in Great Britain for "Topical Resources", Educational Publishers, P.O. Box 329, Broughton, Preston, Lancashire PR3 5LT (Telephone / Fax 01772 863158), by T.Snape & Company Ltd, Boltons Court, Preston, Lancashire.

Typeset by Topical Resources.

ISBN 1 872977 28 6

Introduction

This book has grown from a series of Art Workshops organised by Pisces - a specialist Art supplier. The workshops were organised to help Primary teachers learn basic skills in Drawing, Painting, Printing, Textiles, 3D, Sketchbook and Display. The course providers all have extensive experience of teaching Art in Primary Schools. The book is seen as a tool to help teachers plan their own Art work and as a resource for Art Co-ordinators to help them plan a whole school curriculum.

Contents

Drawing

Drawing is a fundamental activity that is concerned with visual expression and communication. It contributes much to learning through the process of intensive looking, selecting and organising visual material. It is an immediate and direct means of making a visual response to the world that is personal and unique. In drawing we represent in one set of materials what exists in a different set. Drawing can be used for different purposes which fit into four main categories. (Art 7 -11 Schools Council Art Committee)

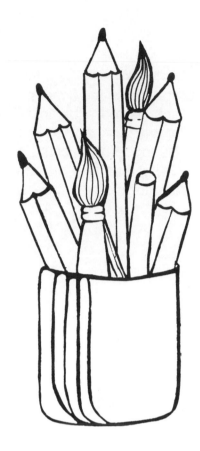

•As a means of **recording** - personal statements from first hand observation. In this work children need to be encouraged to spend as much time **looking** as drawing.

•As **analysis** - isolating certain elements, texture, pattern etc. and focusing attention on them e.g. tonal patterns on shells.

•As **expression** - a personal response to things seen, heard, or imaginary events-poetry, dance, music, drama etc. can lead to expressive drawing.

•As **communication** - when drawing is used to pass on specific information to another person e.g. signs, cartoons, maps etc.

Each of these approaches to drawing will involve children in the use of lines, tones, colours, textures, pattern and shapes working with a range of drawing media on a variety of surfaces.

Drawing is a process that involves a great deal of exploration and experimentation. It involves the working out and thinking about ideas - using a sketch book at KS2 - and discussion with both the teacher and other children about their work and that of other artists.

The best support to drawing is a teacher who generates careful looking through discussion and questions using the language of art to heighten children's awareness of the qualities of the stimulus material or the media they are going to use.

It is essential to offer a range of drawing materials that enable children to explore and experiment in order to discover their characteristics and in turn to use the experience to select what will be most suitable for a future drawing e.g. if children are drawing feathers a fine pen might be appropriate - charcoal might be better for buildings etc. Teachers need to watch for opportunities to encourage personal control of the media - to name it, describe it, hold it and use it. To heighten the awareness of the other possibilities the media might have - using different surfaces, altering pressure, smudging, combining with other media e.g. overdrawing on a painting to add detail. We need to talk with the children about their discoveries, to share them with others and to include these discoveries and comments in displays of work.

Different drawing materials have different

qualities- the following are examples of the range most frequently purchased by school.

They are grouped according to their main characteristics. Ideally children should work with drawing media from every group.

Drawing Media

•**Hard and pointed** - biros, felt tip pens, handwriting pens, HB- 2B pencils, mapping pens and ink.
•**Soft** - pencil crayons, oil pastels, wax crayons, graphite sticks, 4B - 6B pencils.
•**Smudgy** - chalk, chalk pastels, charcoal, charcoal pencils.
•**Wet** - water soluble coloured pencils and crayons, water colour, powder and ready mix paint, inks, "Brusho" dye, thick and thin brushes (round and flat ended).

As drawing concerns mark making almost anything could be included on this list - sand, clay, twigs, torn paper, thread/yarns, wire, and computers! etc. The educational catalogues offer a wide range of drawing media. A carefully chosen limited range from each category will offer the children a variety in their approach to drawing as they progress through school.
•**Papers** - Free Art 80 - 120 gsm, pastel paper, cartridge paper, sugar paper (grey, buff, brown, olive, cream, black), water colour paper.

Paper generally will need to be A4/A3 but occasionally larger or smaller depending on what is to be drawn. It can be used either portrait or landscape according to the subject.

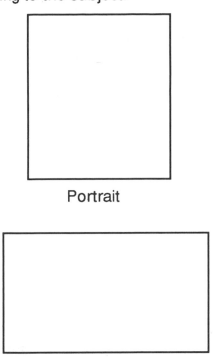

Portrait

Landscape

Drawing employs visual elements (line, tone etc.) to create images. The next section gives a number of suggestions for skill building activities that will encourage children to investigate, explore and experiment with these using a range of drawing media - plus extension work focusing on a range of stimulus material including the work of other artists.

Line

Lines are marks that create on paper shape, pattern, texture and volume. They indicate movement, give direction, form decoration, divide areas and communicate ideas and feelings.

Drawing media - biro, paint and brushes (thick/thin), chalk, pencils, wax crayon, charcoal.

• Choose one media and draw in response to words dictated by the teacher e.g. a bumpy line, a busy line, a tired line etc. Remember it is a personal response - there are many types of bumpy lines!

• Draw a collection of your own lines and the words that describe them.

As a group activity allow each child in turn to draw a line on the same piece of paper - long or short, thick or thin using a range of media. Repeat - each turn requires a new  line from each child. Lines can be drawn next to each other but should not cross. When their are plenty of lines on the paper encourage children to work freely, no longer taking turns - to use any part of the paper to match and extend the lines already there. Continue until the paper is full.

• Draw a collection of lines on half a piece of paper - give it to your neighbour to continue the lines by carefully matching them.

• Match and continue the marks found in part of a line d r a w i n g - taken from a m a g a z i n e, newspaper or artist's work.

• Match the lines on a photocopy of e.g. 1/2 a feather to complete it. Next draw a feather from observation.

• Draw one type of line (zig zag, curved) diagonally across a piece of paper. Make the same line again next to it, in the same direction but in a different media.

Continue using d i f f e r e n t drawing media each time. Talk about the way in which the line changes.

• Stick or print a shape in the centre of a piece of paper. Work round this shape following its outline but using a different line each time. Use a range of drawing media.

• Draw thick and thin lines across the paper - at first close together then gradually getting further apart.

• Draw lines
- falling from the top to the bottom of the paper.
- rising from a pile and floating off.
- wriggling together through a small gap.
- marching in a pattern like an army.

Link this work to P.E./music/drama.

• In P.E./drama move as e.g. an angry sea, then as a quiet warm sea. Draw line patterns that suggest these movements.

• Look for and collect line patterns - around the classroom, on objects, textiles etc. - describe the lines, group the lines collected e.g. curved, zig-zag, wavy, s t r a i g h t, d i a g o n a l, vertical, parallel.

• Make a class list of line words.

- Draw lines in response to sounds e.g. traffic.
- Draw lines in response to music - rhythms.
- Look for different types of lines in the work of other artists using a view finder - collect and describe these lines - using these lines in a drawing of your own "in the style of".

A viewfinder helps children to isolate sections of what may be detailed and complex images. It is better if the window has a large area of frame around it so that the rest of the picture (or object) is hidden. This prevents children being distracted and

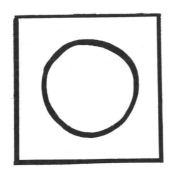

helps them to 'focus in'. The 'window' may be different shapes and sizes depending on the purpose of the work. If the viewfinder is circular the children will find it easier to work on a circular piece of paper.

- **Stimulus Material - visual aids**

Feathers, dried grasses, twigs, skeleton leaves, red cabbage, bird cages, railings, pylons, cranes, rope, toys, ribbon, yarn, baskets, bicycle wheels etc.

- **Artists whose work shows strong linear qualities.**

Van Geogh, Kandinsky, Huntertwasser, Kline, Munch, Bridget Riley, Matisse. Aboriginal bark drawings, African wire sculpture.

Tone

Tone in art refers to the range of values from dark to light usually represented in a scale from black through grey to white. It can depict light and shade, make objects in two dimensional drawings appear three dimensional. Tone can be made by line or areas of colour. Tone can create mood and atmosphere e.g. a haunted house.

Drawing Media:

chalk, chalk pastel, charcoal, ink, paint, thick and thin brushes, grey or black sugar paper.

- Look for and discuss light and dark places in the class-room. Compare the children's hair colour -arrange in groups of light hair / dark hair plus the shades in between.

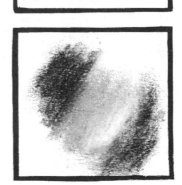

- Using white chalk and char-coal to make light and dark patches on grey paper

- smudge them together - what happens when they meet?

- Explore making further shades of grey.

- Look for shades of grey in newspaper black and white photographs.

- Work on a triangular piece of paper - work

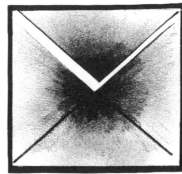

7

from the apex to the opposite side starting dark and getting lighter. This is an effective display if a group of children work this way. Discuss the effect of the light and dark areas.

• Make patterns in black and shades of grey on maths paper. Use only a pencil to make the different tones.

• Choose or cut a shaped piece of grey paper - make it dark on one edge getting lighter towards the opposite - discuss and describe.

• Look at a collection of white shapes with a light shining on them - where are the shadows? Draw the shapes and their shadows.

• Collect pictures showing shadows and objects that give off light. Draw the object - the light - and finally the shadows.

• Look at and discuss book illustrations and the work of other artists - find the lightest and darkest parts in the pictures - on clothing, in doorways, etc.

• Collect black and white photographs of faces - look, discuss and record the lightest and darkest areas.

• Draw a portrait of your friend or an imaginary portrait starting in the middle of the face and working outwards - where do the shadows appear?

• Draw or paint light and dark pictures in response to descriptions in stories e.g. the B.F.G.

• Use line to create tone. Draw straight, curved and crossing lines close together and apart. Draw a shape like a sleeve or crumpled piece of cloth - add extra lines to create folds i.e. the ins and outs.

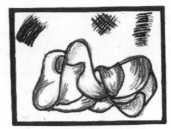

Stimulus Material - visual aids

Shoes, bark, kettles, tools, shells, rocks, bones, pine cones, bottles etc. plus black and white photographs of buildings and faces.

Artists whose work shows strong tonal qualities

The tonal drawings of George Seurat, Renaissance artists, Picasso's 'Guernica', Braques early cubist paintings, Caravaggio and Rembrandt. African masks and sculptures.

Texture

Texture refers to the surface quality of things. It is both man made and natural, functional and decorative and can be tactile or visual. The texture of materials can be changed with use if it is woven or moulded.

Drawing Media.

Wax crayon, soft pencils, charcoal, paint, junk materials.

• Make a collection of objects with different textures - sort, match, describe.

• Make a class list of texture words e.g. rough, woven, smooth, bubbly, spiky, pitted, crinkly, furry etc.

• Collect samples of textures that match these words.

• Feel and describe e.g. a rough texture - draw a 'rough' mark - add further 'rough' marks. Repeat using a different texture as a stimulus.

• Make a rubbing of a rough texture - make a drawing next to your rubbing that matches and copies its texture.

• Print a soft texture - using net, sponge or a paper towel - make a drawing next to your

print that matches and copies its texture.

• Use rubbed and printed textures for collage work:

- to match the textures on a bird or animal

- to create an imaginary bird or animal.

• Collect three different textures e.g. moss, feathers and draw to

show their differences - the textures not the objects.

• Look closely - using a viewfinder - at part of e.g. a pineapple - carefully record the texture on the part you see.

Move the viewfinder and collect the texture from somewhere

else. Next draw the outline shape of the whole pineapple and add the texture.

• In the same way look closely at the texture on part of e.g. a cauliflower next to the pineapple - add the texture.

Stimulus Material - visual aids

Feathers, bark, moss, furry toys, pebbles, shells, textiles, fruit, seeds, vegetables, pictures of buildings and landscapes.

Artists whose work shows strong textural qualities

Dutch still life paintings, Klee, Bacon, Pollock, Chagall, Rauschenberg.

Shape

Shape and form are often used interchangeably. In art however shape is more correctly used to refer to two dimensional outlines. Shape identifies objects, can be regular and irregular, it creates patterns and shows movement and scale.

Drawing Media

Wax crayon, pencil, pen, felt tip, biros.

• Look at, discuss and

describe shapes around the room.

• Make a class collection of the shapes seen on a large piece of paper.

• Make individual shape collections in drawing using a collection of e.g. keys, spoons, leaves etc. from a 'shape' box.

•Invent a new shape with an unusual outline using bits from some of the shapes you have already drawn, and new bits of your own to make a shape with an un-usual outline.

•Draw a large shape with small shapes inside, outside, next to.

•Draw outline shapes of hands, feet, fruit and vegetables.

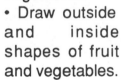

• Draw outside and inside shapes of fruit and vegetables.

• Draw the outline shape of the school - add shapes to it inside and out - large and small.

• Record repeating shapes that are in the environment and use those repeating shapes to make a pattern.

• Draw the spaces between, under and inside shapes that will reveal a shape e.g. a chair.

Stimulus Material - visual aids
Keys, bottles, flags, textiles, teapots, flowers and plants, shoes, toys, tools, kitchen utensils.
Artists who work has strong spatial qualities.
Matisse, O'Keeffe, Magritte, Mondrian, Russeau, Klee.

Pattern and Colour

Pattern and colour are visual elements that also play a part in the introduction of drawing skills.

Pattern - can disguise, communicate, change surfaces, be accidental or intentional. Patterns can be radial, spiral or repeat. They can form borders and designs that in many cases are cultural in origin and tradition.

Colour - can transform, be limited, change moods and opinions. It is both natural and man made - complimentary and contrasting. It can be mixed, matched and blended. Some colours have a special meaning that evoke images and ideas e.g. a blue mood.

Each child handles materials, thinks feels and imagines in an individual way which we as teachers must foster and encourage. The thinking and expressing of new ideas, the recording and responding to what is seen are all important as are the exploration and control of media and the sharing and appreciation of their own work and that of others. Drawing activities should be planned in such a way to foster, encourage and develop these in a progressive non threatening way.

Painting

It is true to say, that in the western art tradition (European in particular), there has been a hierarchy of art forms which has placed painting at the top. The walls of our galleries are lined with framed images and our art colleges are still full of young people engaging in this same activity. The history of painting can be traced back to the walls of caves and tombs. Today, although many continue the 'traditional' approach, the boundaries of painting are being pushed in terms of content, concept and the materials that are being used.

Young children seem to effortlessly combine using the paintbrush as a drawing tool and as a more expressive means of conveying their ideas and feelings. This natural inclination needs to be harnessed early and they need to be provided with a framework of skills and techniques that will enable them to become independent in making the most appropriate choices.

Continuity and Progression

Without careful planning, it is unlikely that continuity and progression will naturally occur in any area of artistic experience. End of Key Stage Descriptions indicate the types and range of performance that the majority of children should characteristically demonstrate by the end of the Key Stage but they do not suggest a framework for achieving these ends.

Painting, is one of a range of artistic experiences that children will encounter in the Primary phase and one well suited to delivering the requirements of both attainment targets.

The Programme of Study for both Key Stages stipulates many areas where "pupils should be taught" or "pupils should be introduced to.....".The practical activity of painting will allow the pupils to fulfil the requirements of these areas.

Pupils engage in painting activities that enable them to work individually, in groups or even on a whole class project such as a mural. They are able to express ideas and feelings in paint as well as making observations and images. Ideas, meanings and feelings are communicated in visual form yet at the same time, pupils will also be developing a critical vocabulary to articulate their views. The visual elements of art (e.g. line, tone, colour etc.) will be reinforced through practical activity and through consideration of the work of other artists. In this way, the relationship between making and appraising will be understood and developed from an early age.

Initial considerations when planning for progression may centre, in particular, around four areas;

• The range of paint on offer.
• The range of applicators used.
• The range of paper made available.
• The variety of stimulus / starting points.

These areas will be considered in greater detail when classroom planning and organisation becomes the focus.

However, consideration can be given to the progression of some associated skills which begin with children's first experiences, probably in the home, nursery or reception class and develop through to their final year in Key Stage Two.

Progression of Skills, Nursery to Year Six

Using fingers/ hands... to ....Fine manipulation of tools.

Using ready-mixed paint.... to ....Ability to mix and alter the consistency of a range of paints.

Working with Primary... Secondary.. Tertiary...... Subtle shades and tones colours

Continual development of a more sophisticated vocabulary.

Flat areas of colour....... to ....Implied texture.

A more detailed progression can be found on the opposite page.

Painting Progression through the Primary School

Nursery
Children should explore a wide variety of paint using a range of applicators. They should try out a range of simple tools and be encouraged to use their hands, feet and fingers. They should experience painting flat and upright on a varity of coloured and shaped paper. Collecting and mixing colours will also help in building a colour vocabulary.

Reception
Children can experiment with mixing different textures into paint to change the consistency. There should be repetition and consolidation of nursery skills so that no children 'miss out'. Children should start to name specific colours and may be introduced to colours through the computer.

Year 1
Continuing with the experimentation, children need to gain greater control over the range of applicators used. They need to explore how the consistency can be altered by the addition of water alone. Increasing the use of colour vocabulary may lead to exploration of hues for example, creating bright and dull primary colours.

Year 2
Children should know and name primary and secondary colours. They should experiment with combining secondary colours to form different browns, (tertiary colours). They should have looked at how artists have used colour and have experimented with some of their techniques. Children could be encouraged to include other media into their paintings.

Year 3
Children may need some revision of colour theory developed so far. They may then explore areas such as links between colour and feelings. If possible, different paints and applicators could be introduced or new ways with familiar materials demonstrated. Exploration of warm and cool colours will further enhance knowlege of colour theory.

Year 4
As many colours can now be achieved, switch focus to Tone and look at Monochrome. Make a particular focus on how painting is tackled in other cultures or from a particular period. Children need to be set challenges where they have to make informed choices and be encouraged to sustain a piece of work over a period of time.

Year 5
Children should develop a particular theme and work from sketching through modification to a final product. Consider exhibiting finished work. After considering established artists' work, look particularly at the use of fore, middle and backgrounds. Consider perspective and also deliberate distortion. Look at different portraits and consider creating skin tones.

Year 6
Childn should study a particular artist or movement and make use of this knowledge in their own work. Children could explore how painting provides an insight into social and historical situations as well as conveying feelings. They should be encouraged, through selection and reflection, to build up a folio of work demonstrating progression of knowledge and understanding.

Classroom Organisation and Management

Available budget unfortunately plays a large role in selecting the range of art materials that are made available to children. However, the old maxim that "you get what you pay for" still holds true when considering materials for painting.

If paint made from good quality pigment is purchased, then successful secondary colours **can** be made (yes, even purple!). Advocating the use of **Red, Blue, Yellow, Black and White** alone, not only saves money, but provides a more creative challenge to children in terms of mixing their own colours. As children become proficient, you may consider introducing a **'dual primary'** set of colours where a'warm'and 'cool' version of each primary colour provides greater scope for colour mixing and, especially, matching.

Where possible, children should have opportunities to experience a range of media including: powder, ready-mix, acrylic and tempera paint. A smaller quantity of a wide range would be preferable and this remains true when considering both applicators and painting papers.

When children use the work of established painters as a starting point, experimenting with a **range** of tools and materials is the only way they can begin to understand aspects of a painter's style.

Painting activities need to plan for the use of a range of **paint, applicators, papers and starting points.**

Assuming that you are fortunate enough to have access to this range, consideration needs to be given to the accessibility of materials.

• How is access arranged?

• How independent are the children able to be?

• Is there space to work large?

• Can they work flat / on easels?

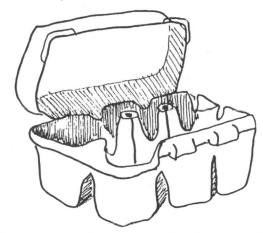

Sometimes the most effective solutions are creative rather than costly! Egg boxes provide an excellent receptacle for powder colour that can be easily stacked when not in use. I have seen infants effectively managing a system of red, blue, two yellows, (you seem to get through twice as much) black and white in an egg box. The children are shown how to load a wet bush with dry powder and then mix this on a flat palette.

Other advantages of powder colour include being able to mix it with a variety of other things e.g. sand or P.V.A.glue.

Having a range of materials, well organised and accessible is the key to providing the kind of environment that will encourage young people across the key stages to want to experiment in this area of art experience.

WATER
CLEAN BRUSH
DRY POWDER PAINT
FLAT MIXING PALETTE

Colour

Although children sometimes choose or are directed to work in monochrome, it is the opportunity to work in and experiment with colour that makes painting so exciting. Early experimentation usually revolves around colour mixing and progresses to more sophisticated colour matching.

Initially, children are transfixed by the seemingly magical transformation that takes place when two colours are mixed.

Even the act of cleaning brushes in a water jar can become an occasion to reinforce colour theory.

As they begin to master the relationship between the process and the product, they will need to begin having more control in the mixing and setting some kind of colour matching challenge is the ideal way of doing this.

Children can be encouraged to compare and contrast the range of colours to be found in both nature and the made environment. They can then be asked to explore how a variety of artists have chosen to incorporate colour into their work.

The scientific theory of colour can prove to be a challenging topic even for adults, but children need to be encouraged from the outset to select the appropriate vocabulary when discussing their observations. Teachers need to be clear in their own understanding of terms such as; tone, shade, hue, intensity etc.

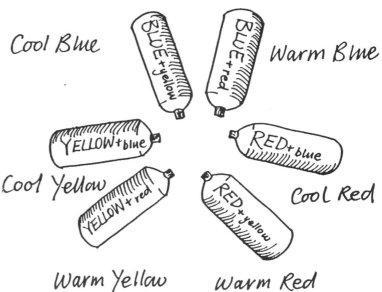

Cool Blue   Warm Blue

YELLOW+blue

Cool Yellow   RED+blue   Cool Red

YELLOW+red   RED+yellow

Warm Yellow   Warm Red

Shading - light to dark

As already mentioned, by offering only the primary colours, children will be stimulated to experiment with creating the most appropriate colours for their needs.

'River Landscape with a boat' by George Pierre Seurat (1859-91)
Private Collection/Peter Willi/Bridgeman Art Library, London

River Landscape with a boat - George Seurat - (1859 -1891)
Reproduced with kind permission from Peter Willi / Bridgeman Art Library

Seurat was a master of optical colour mixing e.g. using red and yellow dots to create the effect of orange.

USING ARTISTS' WORK

There is no real substitute for exposing children to original works of art. Despite the fact that there are some really good reproductions available to buy and in some cases, to borrow, nothing can really be a substitute for the experience of sheer scale, texture and just a sense of 'occasion' that an art space can give to a work.

After viewing art works, children need to be guided in discussion by plenty of open ended questions that promote a more considered use of descriptive vocabulary. Teachers should aim to introduce new words regularly and then facilitate opportunities where children can consolidate their knowledge both verbally and in written forms if appropriate.

COLOUR

The artists palette, What colours have been used?
How have they been made?

colour
composition
inspiration
perspective
light
line
texture

HOW DO YOU FEEL ABOUT THIS WORK OF ART?

APPLICATION

How has the paint actually been put on? Is the surface smooth or rough? has anything other than paint been used?

For children to appreciate and understand what might be considered an artist's style, they will need to explore areas that include: use of colour, method of application, treatment of background and composition.

These four areas could be tackled in four separate lessons or spread out over a longer period of time. The experimental work could be linked to work in sketchbooks or could form part of a display that demonstrates both process and product.

What is critical, is providing an opportunity for the children to demonstrate exactly what they have understood about an artist's style.

A group of children may start off by looking at a range of work by Lowry for example. Having discussed, experimented with and explored aspects of his treatment of colour, application, background and composition, they are ready to be challenged with a task that will enable them to demonstrate what they have learned. Some exploration of an artist's work may involve an element of copying either all or part of a work. This is fine as a starting point as long as it provides the children with an opportunity to discover about an artist's way of working that they can then utilise for their own ends.

A class that had experimented with Lowry's style might be given a task that involves them looking at children in the playground, making observational sketches and then, supported by photographs of their friends at play, make their own paintings of children at play in the style of Lowry.

This type of activity, will not only help the children explore their developing understanding but will also provide some 'evidence' that could form the basis for assessment.

THOMAS MANNING

BACKGROUND

Imagine the picture without any people or objects. What are you left with?

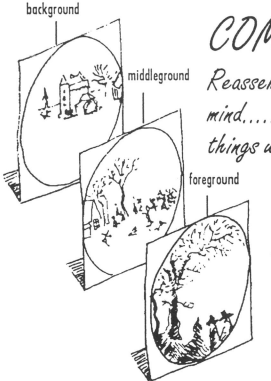

background

middleground

foreground

COMPOSITION

Reassemble the picture in your mind..... why has the artist put things where they are?

Would they look as good somewhere else?

Textiles

The use of Textiles and 'crafts' linked to textiles can contribute to childrens' sensory and aesthetic development and provide a wealth of rich and exciting experiences for Key Stage 1 and Key Stage 2 primary children.

Children can explore Textiles from an historical, geographical, scientific, technological and artistic way linking their investigations to mathematics and encompassing the whole primary curriculum.

Pupils can create their own designs gaining inspiration from times throughout history e.g. Tudor, Viking or Celtic traditional symbols.

Other cultures can influence designs and many countries' styles and traditions can be used to help pupils evolve their own images once existing patterns have been observed and recorded.

From a scientific point of view the pupils can investigate woven and non woven materials, natural and man made fabrics and the changes that take place in fibres when they are dyed and combined. Tests can be carried out for strength, warmth and whether they are waterproof or not.

For Design Technology the fabrics and fibres should be measured, shaped, combined and finished to produce an article or product which could be a wall hanging, container, cushion, slippers, curtain fabric etc.

For the artistic element, pattern, colour, tone and texture should be explored. Existing patterns can be enhanced or white/plain coloured fabric can be coloured and patterned using other cultures as inspiration or designs inspired by historical times which would give the pupils confidence and help them create their own images.

Above all textiles work is fun and children and adults alike can create exciting and interesting products of a high quality when the area is explored fully and sufficient time is allowed.

N.B. It is important that all fabrics are washed before any painting, dyeing or decoration is applied as often fabric is coated with substances which will resist change.

The following techniques will enable you to plan your Textiles work linked to other curriculum areas and although suggestions are made as to finished products, the skills can be applied to various activities.

Weaving

Weaving is an activity that can be taught to very young children in its simplest form yet because of the variety of looms and materials, it will excite and stimulate pupils from Key Stage 1 and Key Stage 2. The following techniques are listed in order of complexity and yet if Key Stage 2 pupils have had no previous experience in weaving it is appropriate to introduce them to the simplest form first. The simplest form of weaving involves an adult prepared card weaving frame which has vertical straight cuts in it. Through this card weaving frame, the children weave card strips in a variety of colours in an under and over technique. The children should cut the strips of card to give them practice in cutting skills.

The colours chosen can be on a theme e.g. Autumn or shades of one colour or the choice can be left entirely to the pupils.

A small step forwards from this technique could be adult prepared cards with wavy

or zig-zag vertical cuts. The introduction of a wider range of materials for weaving will enable the pupils to select textures as well as colours leading to more interesting weavings. Try Artstraws, strips of sugar paper, wrapping paper, wallpaper, newspapers, magazines etc. Once the weavings have been created they can be mounted in card frames to

create the fronts of greetings cards, laminated for place mats or glued onto a backing and cut into a simple shape which can then be attached to the front of a card.

A notched loom is the next step. These can be purchased from Educational Suppliers or made from reclaimed card and come in a variety of shapes and sizes: squares, rectangles and circles.

The squares and rectangles are threaded in the same way. Knot onto one of the points a piece of yarn for the vertical threads - the warps. Wrap around the pointed end first at the top and then at the bottom of the loom alternately until the loom is fully warped. It is important that the threads are

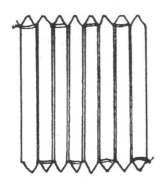

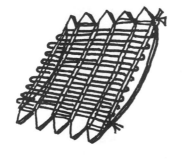

pulled quite tightly so that the card loom becomes slightly bowed, this will make the weaving easier. It is important to

introduce a plastic bodkin to the children to enable them to weave the weft threads - the horizontal threads - through the warp and so create a piece of woven fabric. The yarns for the weft can be extremely varied in texture, thickness and colour e.g. wool, cotton, ribbon, lace, silk etc

To remove a square or rectangular weaving from its frame, simply slip the loops from around the notches and thread a piece of dowel through the loops to form a rigid support pole at the top and the bottom of a small wall hanging. Alternatively tassels can be made and attached to the loops to create a mat.

The circular loom is made up as in the diagram, threading the warp yarn around the outside

notches and through the centre hole alternately going to the diagonally opposite notch in a star formation. Begin the weaving at the centre and move outwards in a circular motion until the frame is covered. The circular weaving is removed from the frame by slipping the loops from around the notches and either ribbon threaded through or tassels added.

Bicycle wheels make interesting circular weaving frames, the spokes becoming the warp 'thread', however although an interesting hanging can be created by adding braids and tassels etc. it is impossible to remove the weaving from its loom.

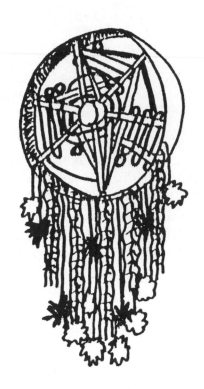

Lower Key Stage 2 pupils can create their own looms using a shoe box, carpet tape and lolly sticks. The lolly sticks can be glued to opposite ends of the shoe box, either the short or the long sides yet they must be secured firmly with carpet tape placed over them to ensure that under strain from the warp threads the lolly sticks are not pulled off. One end of the warp thread should be tied to one of

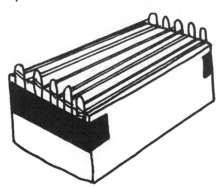

the corner lolly sticks and wrapped around the lolly sticks alternately from one end to the other. A shuttle can be

created from thick card to thread the weft

yarns over and under the warp or a plastic bodkin can be used.

At upper Key Stage 2 the pupils can make a weaving loom from 4 pieces of strip wood and triangulated corner strengtheners glued on the front and the back of the corners of the square or rectangular frame. Drilled holes can be

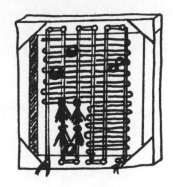

made to place pieces of dowel in to attach the warp thread or panel pins can be used. The children are now taking full control over the size and shape of their weaving and to assist in this independence an extremely wide range of materials should be provided in a variety of colours e.g. ribbon, threads of different materials, wools, strips of fabric, pipe cleaners, tinsel etc.

The weaving is removed from the loom by unhooking the warp threads from the dowel or panel pins and dowel or square section wood threaded through the loops to create a stable wallhanging. To complete the wallhanging braids, tassels, finger knitting, feathers, sequins and beads can be attached by sewing or gluing to the finished piece of woven fabric.

Braids and Knitting

There are many types of knitting suitable for Key Stage 2 pupils all of which can be created using a wide variety of textures and width of yarns.

Finger Knitting

A slip knot is created and this is the first 'stitch' which should be placed on the forefinger. Wrap the yarn around the same finger pulling it tight and and pull the first stich over the second tightening the yarn when the stitch has been made.

Continue until there is a long strand made.

Four Finger Knitting

Create a slip knot and place it over the forefinger wrapping the yarn around the next three fingers in an under and over way creating the first row of 'stitches'. On the next row, wrap the yarn around the fingers in the same way and then pull the first row of stitches over the second. Continue until a strip of knitted fabric has been created.

Bobbin Knitting

A Bobbin is a piece of wood which has a wide circular hole through the centre and to create the stitches, panel pins should be hammered into the top rim. The yarn is wrapped around the top pins once to create the first row of 'stitches', a second row of stitches is placed around the panel pins and the first row of stitches is then pulled off the pins over the second row. A narrow tube of stitches will move down the central hole

of the bobbin and the rows should be continued until a long strand has been created. This can then be coiled to create a mat or applied onto fabric creating a raised effect.

God's Eyes(Ojo de Dio's)

These are creative wrappings around a star shaped frame of 4 or 6 points which can be created out of twigs, dowel, square section wood, strip wood or lolly sticks and is suitable for pupils from Year 2 upwards. First create the star frame by fastening the sticks together at the centre with sticky tape, glue or by wrapping with thread or yarn.

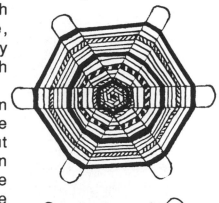

A length of yarn should be selected about one metre in length and one end should be tied to the centre of the star. It is then wrapped around the arms of the frame in a circular fashion

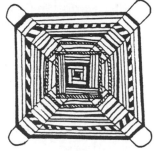

going under and then over the arms which will increase the size of the pattern from the centre outwards. When a new piece of yarn is needed simply tie onto the end of the last piece and continue until the desired effect has been achieved.

Once the God's Eye has been created, the pupils can choose which side is to be the front and which

is to be the back as the two sides are different in design. Trim the ends of the knots and the God's Eyes can have tassels attached or depending on their size they can become hangings, greetings cards fronts, Christmas Decorations or jewellery.

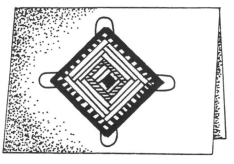

Wrapping

Wrapping is a technique that can use any yarns, threads, ribbons and silk to create an item that is covered with the children's chosen textures, patterns and colours. Wrapping a rectangular piece of reclaimed card is the easiest method and can be introduced to Key Stage 1 pupils. An essential piece of equipment is double sided sellotape.

The rectangular piece of reclaimed card should have one piece of double sided tape placed the full length of its reverse side lengthways.

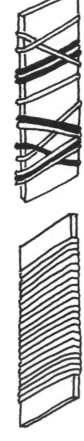

This will be used to attach the ends of the threads to and will ensure that the wrapping will not slip. Cut a piece of thread approx-imately one metre in length and attach one end to the tape. Wrap around the piece of card pulling the thread tight. Young children should be encouraged to choose their own threads and may wrap randomly whereas older pupils may be required to wrap in a more orderly fashion to create stripes and patterns. When the first piece of thread is finished, the end should be attached to the double sided tape and a second piece of thread chosen.

Repeat the process until the child is satisfied with the design or all the double sided tape is

covered. The piece of wrapped card can be glued to the front of a greetings card and a flame added to create a quality card which is individual in colour choice pattern and texture.

This technique can be used by Key Stage 2 pupils to record colour choices for a weaving, collage or tapestry and the strip can be placed into a sketch book or onto a design board.

Any simple 2D shape can be wrapped as long as the card is thick and does not bend when the threads are pulled tight and the essential double sided tape is used.

3D shapes can be wrapped to create containers, gift boxes and Christmas Decorations.

Painting

Paints that are used on paper can also be used on textiles. However, if the fabric item produced needs to be washed, then fabric paints should be used and the manufacturers instructions followed regarding the fixing of the paints.

The children can experiment with ways of attaching the fabric to be coloured securely to the table top by either masking tape or pins or by stretching the fabric to be painted on a frame to stop the fabric wrinkling when painted.

There are a range of different pieces of equipment that can be experimented with on paper before being used on fabric and these include bristle brushes of different shapes and sizes, sponge rollers and sponge brushes to create textured effects.

A sprayed effect can be created by using a spray diffuser filled with 60% paint to 40% water. Other items such as nailbrushes and toothbrushes can give similar effects when coated in paint and 'flicked'.

Most of the techniques are suitable for Key Stage 1 and Key Stage 2 pupils. It is the application of skills, finished article and teacher expectation that will vary according to the age of the pupils.

3D Paints

3D Paints give extra effect to certain pieces of work. They are available in 4 types, glossy, glitter, pearl and puff and when dry they have a three dimensional texture. They are easy to use yet quite expensive and they should therefore be used for small areas, adding detail to patterns. Pupils should discuss their design with an adult in order to justify their use.

Drawing

Pupils can draw directly on to material using fabric pastels or felt pens. Instructions for their use and setting are clearly explained on the packaging and although inexpensive it helps if pupils design on paper first and then trace their design onto fabric. If an observational drawing has been made of a leaf for example, tracing the drawing onto fabric will enable the pupils to create a repeat pattern using the same image.

Transfers

Pupils can create their own transfers by using fabric wax crayons. The design must be drawn onto paper using the crayons - press on to apply a lot of wax. Turn the finished design face downwards onto the plain coloured fabric and iron onto the reverse side of the paper pressing down firmly for about thirty seconds until the design has been transferred onto the fabric. An adult must use the iron which should be on a hot setting. Before removing the paper, carefully lift a corner of the drawn design to check the colour strength of the transfer. If it is not bright enough then iron for a few seconds more until it has transferred to your satisfaction.

Remember! Any lettering on the design must be in reverse on the paper transfer to appear the right way round when ironed onto the fabric.

Marbling

To transfer a marbled effect onto fabric purchase textile marbling inks and marbling medium. The marbling medium is mixed with water forming a gel similar to wall paper paste. The medium must be placed in the bottom of a shallow tray and the marbling inks dripped onto its surface. A pattern can be created in the inks using a paintbrush, afro comb or feather to drag the inks and then the fabric should be laid onto the surface of the gel, gently pressed and when removed the marbled pattern will have transferred onto the fabric.

Image Transferring

'Image Maker' can be used to transfer photocopies or pages from magazines onto fabrics or items of clothing and is a technique suitable for Key Stage 2 pupils. The children can draw or paint a design to be transferred. A monochrome pattern will be easy to photocopy whereas a painting would need to be photocopied on a colour photocopier. The image must be covered with image maker using a brush and then placed image side down onto the fabric. Press the image down firmly by using a roller on the reverse side of the paper and then allow to dry fully. To remove the paper and reveal the image, soak the paper backing with water and gently rub away the paper with a sponge. When all the paper has been removed, coat the image with a thin coat of image maker and allow to dry.

Remember! Any lettering on the design must be in reverse to appear the right way round when transferred onto the fabric.

Printing

Printing onto textiles using natural or man made objects enables the pupils to create a repeating pattern. A small amount of the paint should be placed onto a shallow tray and rollered out evenly. The object to be used for printing must be pressed into the paint and then printed onto the fabric using gentle pressure.

Before another print is made, the paint in the tray should be rollered again and the printing object pressed into it enabling prints of a consistent colour to be made. Using the chosen object a variety of patterns can be made e.g. over printing, printing in rows, reverse prints and rotational prints using one colour or several colours. The printing objects should be displayed with the finished work.

Printing Blocks

Pupils can create their own printing blocks very easily by using sticky backed draught excluder attached to aerosol lids, wooden blocks or thick card.

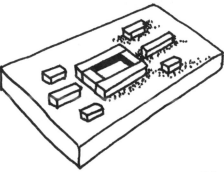

The plastic aerosol lids enable the excluder to be repositioned whereas a design can be drawn onto the wooden blocks and card and the lines of the design followed with the draught excluder.

Press print can be drawn into using a pencil to create a printing block. The whole block can be used or the picture / symbol drawn can be cut from the surround and used as a shaped printing block.

The printing blocks should always be displayed with the final designs to show the starting points.

Draught Proof Strips   Press Print

Screen Printing.

There are many ways of creating a screen for repeat printing of the same image - paper stencil, screen filler method, drawing fluid and photographic emulsion. However primary children should be introduced to the paper stencil method which is suitable for Key Stage 2 pupils. A piece of white newsprint paper should be cut to the size of the inside measurement of the screen and the

image cut out from the centre of the newsprint. Glue brown sticky tape all around the edge of the inside of the screen to prevent seepage of the printing inks. Screen printing inks result in better prints and

inhibit seepage around the edge of the image.

Place the paper stencil onto the fabric in the position required, lay the screen on top of the stencil and place screen printing ink in a line along one edge of the screen well. Using a squeegee, in one fluid movement apply pressure and pull the squeegee towards yourself and then push it away to the opposite edge once more. Carefully lift the screen from the fabric. The stencil will have stuck to the screen. Lay the screen onto the

position required for the next image. Carry on until the piece of fabric is decorated with the desired pattern taking care not to place the screen into any of the wet ink. Wash the screen and dry thoroughly before using again.

Stencilling

For stencilling techniques to be effective the paint must not spread under the objects or image placed onto the fabric. Although heavy objects e.g. coins, marbles, beads etc. can be placed on the fabric and a spray dye lightly used to colour the fabric, an easier and more detailed design can be achieved by using sticky backed plastic to create the image.

Draw the image onto the paper side of the sticky backed plastic and when satisfied cut out the image which could be an animal, abstract shape, letters or any design created by the pupils. Peel off the paper backing from the plastic and stick the image onto plain coloured fabric which can be cotton or polyester cotton. Ensure the image is pressed firmly onto the fabric and then decide on the equipment and colours to be used. Remember that if the fabric is to be washed, fabric colourings should be used. However for an item that does not need washing, ordinary colourings can be used.

Felt pens or pastels can be applied or rollers, sponge brushes and paintbrushes used to apply colour over the image and background fabric. The image should be painted / drawn over, not around.

When the paint is dry remove the sticky backed plastic image and the clean sharp edged design can be enhanced by using 3D paints, sequins etc.

This technique is very effective when creating a class wall hanging as each child can create their own image, attach it to the backing fabric which can then be decorated by the whole class or group of

children. When dry the sticky backed images can be removed individually and the clean images enhanced by the pupils. Suitable subjects for this technique are minibeasts, under the sea and jungle scenes.

Dyeing

Dip and Dye.

Decorating a plain fabric with the dip and dye method is very easy and although it is suitable for Nursery and Key Stage 1 pupils, it can be very effective when used by Key Stage 2 pupils to create a background onto which further decoration can be added.

Dry Fabric Method.

The piece of fabric to be dyed can be folded in a variety of ways and dipped into a variety of dyes. For very young pupils food colourings can be used whereas older children can dye with Dylon dyes which are economical to use or if non of these are available inks will also work.

Method 1.

Fold a square piece of fabric in half, into quarters and then diagonally as you would if you were creating a cut paper snowflake. When folded the fabric will be triangular in shape and the three corners should then be dipped into the dyes. Choose two or three colours. Open the fabric flat immediately and allow to dry on a paper towel or newsprint.

Method 2.

Fold a square or rectangular piece of fabric concertina style from one end to the other. When folded into a strip, fold the strip in half and dip each end into different coloured dyes. Open the fabric flat and allow to dry on an absorbent paper.

Method 3.

Fold a square piece of fabric concertina style diagonally, fold the strip in half and dip each end into different colourings. Open the fabric out flat and allow to dry on an absorbent paper.

These are just three examples of folding techniques. There are many other ways of folding the fabric and the pupils should be encouraged to experiment with their folding and colour combinations.

Wet Fabric Method

The fabric to be dyed is folded in the same way as for the dry fabric method. However, before being dipped into the dyes / colourings, the fabric should be wet thoroughly enabling the dyes to spread further through the water in the fabric creating a diffused edge in contrast to the sharp edges which result from the dry fabric dip and dye method.

Sprinkling

This is a colouring technique that is very easy yet can create stunning effects which can be used as a background and enhanced with 3D paints. Plain coloured fabric must be thoroughly wet and then spread flat onto paper on which it is left to dry after colouring. Easibrush or Brusho watercolour powders are used which are supplied in small tubs because of their concentrated nature. Make holes in the lids of the tubs with a compass point so that the powders can be sprinkled onto the wet fabric. The process is very easy but take care with the colour choices made. The most effective results are gained by using for example hot colours, cold colours, colour families or 2 / 3 contrasting colours. As the powders touch the wet fabric they begin to spread creating pleasing patterns with merging colours and the pupils will be able to see the colour mixing effect - chromatography. This effect is not wash proof. It can be used on cotton, polyester cotton, and linen as well as paper.

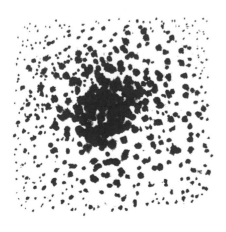

Tie and Dye

Tie and dye is a resist method of dyeing cotton fabrics. The dye cannot penetrate into the cotton under the materials which have been used to hold the fabric. These can be clip pegs, bull dog clips, string or elastic bands.

For young children the use of elastic bands is the easiest method but remember - the elastic bands must be thick and pulled tightly around the cotton! Dylon dyes are effective for colouring the fabric as they are economical to use and come in a variety of colours. The fabric can be tied in many ways to give different effects when dyed.

Starburst Effect

A square of cotton fabric is held at the centre and gathered downwards into a thin strip. Elastic bands are then wrapped tightly around the fabric at intervals. The wrapped fabric should then be fully immersed in the dye and left for at least an hour. When the time has passed the fabric should be removed from the dye and washed in cold  water until the water runs clear at which time the elastic bands can be cut away and the fabric opened out flat and left to dry. The starburst pattern is easy to recognise and can be used on T shirts, cushions, bags etc.

To dye with more than one colour, immerse the tied fabric first in a light dye, rinse until the water runs clear but do

not remove the elastic bands. Add more elastic bands to the wet fabric in the same way as before and then immerse the fabric in a darker coloured dye. When the second hour has elapsed, remove the fabric, rinse and cut away the elastic bands to reveal a two coloured starburst which should be allowed to dry flat.

Ring Effect

Any shape of cotton fabric can be used for this technique as the effect is smaller and more focussed. Place a marble (or similar item e.g. bottle top, bead, button etc.) onto the cotton fabric and gather the cotton around the

marble securing it in place with an elastic band pulled tight. Repeat the process until the cotton has been covered with the number of marbles required and then immerse in the dye. Repeat the dyeing process as for the starburst

effect and when the elastic bands are removed un-dyed rings of the fabric can clearly be seen.

Pleating

A square or rectangular piece of fabric is folded into pleats either diagonally or from side to side and the pleated strip

folded in half. Elastic bands should be wrapped tightly around the cotton at intervals and then the dyeing and rinsing process carried out as described before.

Tied Marbled Effect

Any shape of cotton fabric can be scrunched into a ball and then wrapped tightly with elastic bands. Dye, rinse and dry the fabric as before and when the elastic bands are removed a randomly dyed marbled effect can be seen.

Printmaking

As well as being a chosen medium of expression for practising artists, printmaking is a process led, systematic way of working that most children will be able to successfully develop and express their creative ideas.

The products range from one-off monoprints in monotone or colour to sophisticated multiple images in a range of colours that demonstrate a clear understanding of a range of concepts. A focused study in printing will reveal many cross-curricular links incorporating mathematics, history and opportunities for language work. The ability to produce multiple images can easily be exploited and used to fulfil a particular need which would incorporate additional links with technology. It is important for the non art specialist to become both confident and competent in their practical understanding and application of this area. The process of printing can often best be described through demonstration by the teacher so time spent experimenting is to be highly recommended.

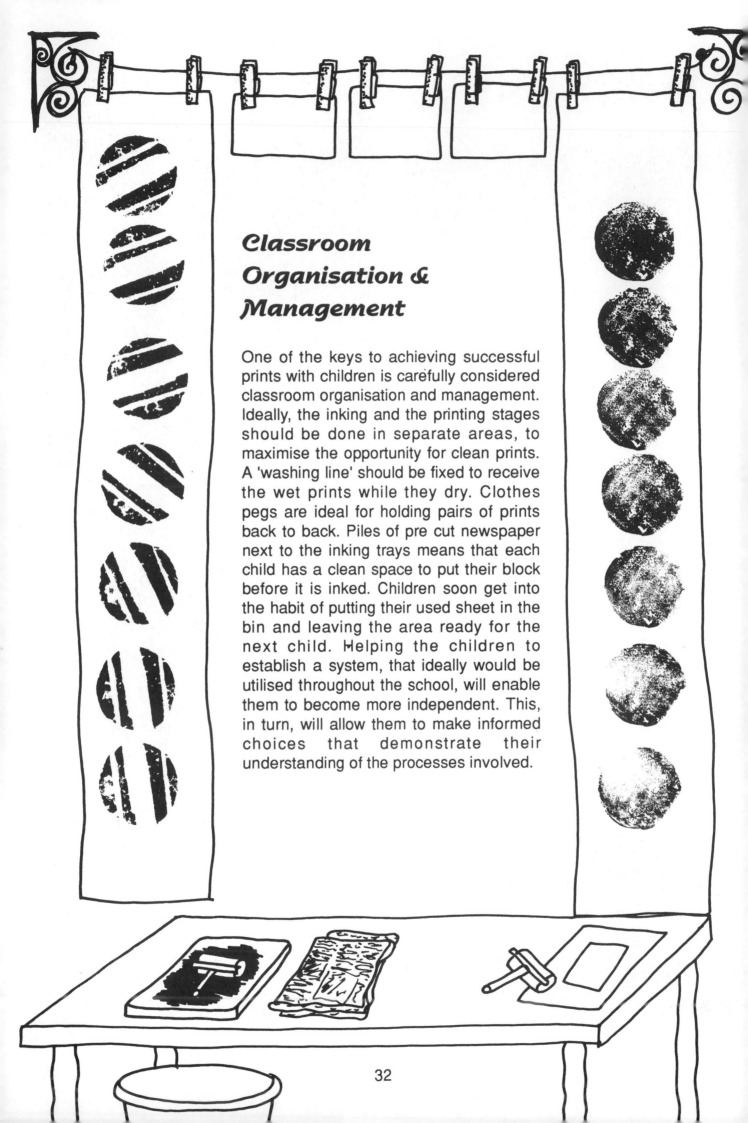

Classroom Organisation & Management

One of the keys to achieving successful prints with children is carefully considered classroom organisation and management. Ideally, the inking and the printing stages should be done in separate areas, to maximise the opportunity for clean prints. A 'washing line' should be fixed to receive the wet prints while they dry. Clothes pegs are ideal for holding pairs of prints back to back. Piles of pre cut newspaper next to the inking trays means that each child has a clean space to put their block before it is inked. Children soon get into the habit of putting their used sheet in the bin and leaving the area ready for the next child. Helping the children to establish a system, that ideally would be utilised throughout the school, will enable them to become more independent. This, in turn, will allow them to make informed choices that demonstrate their understanding of the processes involved.

Vocabulary

Printing, like other skills based activities, has its own accompanying vocabulary. Many excellent books on the subject will explain terms at length and provide useful glossaries. One of the most important terms to be clear about is the distinction between the term 'print' and 'reproduction'. The work that is produced by children engaged in printmaking will be unique and original, no two prints will be exactly alike. The children may be used to looking at reproductions of artists work and calling these 'prints'. Looking at work by established printmakers may help illustrate this point as well as providing a starting point for their own work. Looking at original prints will also enable the children to to continue to explore their understading of the visual elements. Discussing prints in terms of line, tone, colour, texture, shape, form, pattern, or a combination of these will enhance children's understanding of the work of artists in general.

Equipment

There is relatively little needed to set up printmaking in the classroom so it is worth investing in some specific resources.

Although many early experiments can be done using paint, it is best to use a water-based printing ink as soon as possible. The primary colours, black and white will provide children with all they need to create their own range of colours as well as reinforcing colour-mixing 'theory' introduced though painting.

A portable (shareable) printing box may contain various multiples of;

• Water-based printing ink
• Soft rollers (sponge)
• Hard rollers (rubber)
• Inking trays, or glass / perspex sheet
• Stencil brush
• Palette knives
• Pre-cut newspaper

In addition to this, to facilitate the making of printing blocks, you will need to buy or collect;

• Lino and some tools
• Polystyrene printing material
  (Pressprint, Easyprint)
• A range of card and papers
• Fabrics and other collage materials
• Scraps of wood and items to make
  marks with.

Needless to say, many of the resources needed to create printing blocks would be found among general art collections.

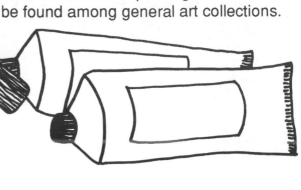

Continuity and Progression

For the children to build up a range of skills, there needs to be progression across the two key stages.

Children will probably start by printing with non absorbent found objects. (Lego bricks, plastic toys and letters etc.)

When they print with absorbent found and prepared objects, (potato, sponge, cork etc.) they will be able to experiment with not inking for each print but to see the repeated pattern gradually fade. Children can also experiment with overlapping and rotation of the object.

At this stage the ink has probably been transferred to the paper by pressing the object directly into the ink. When the children make their own blocks, the ink will almost certainly be transferred by means of a roller onto the block and then this pressed on to the paper. It is at this stage that an organised system needs reinforcing.

35

Children's own blocks may consist of 'collages' that have been well stuck down and sealed with P.V.A. glue, card bases with card or masking tape shapes applied, more traditional lino or its modern equivalent, polystyrene printing medium.

They will need to experiment to discover which materials make successful prints and can be shown, by demonstration, how to make prints from the raised surface of their blocks (relief print) and to obtain a print from the recessed areas of the block (intaglio print).

As a guide to how the final print may appear, the children could be encouraged to make a rubbing with thin paper and a soft pencil or crayon. As well as providing a useful informative stage in the process, this enables the pupil to make changes to the block before it gets wet with inking.

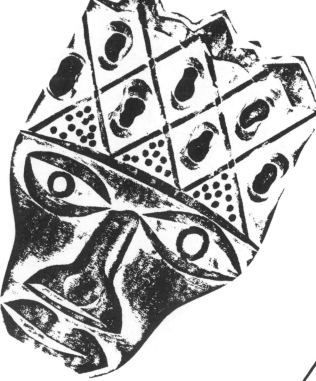

At some stage, the children may be introduced to screen printing. There is much useful experimental work that can be done in exploring stencils and templates before screen printing is attempted and then, the teacher may consider adopting an approach that involves demonstration and group prints. Enabling a whole class to print individually is very time consuming.

Printing Progression Through the Primary School

Nursery

Children wil print using non-absobent found objects and use body parts to print with. They can make simple transfer prints from finger paintings.

Reception

Children can explore the difference when printing with absorbent found and prepared objects. More attention can be given to colour and pattern forming. Children can be encouraged to make rubbings and print onto a variety of surfaces. Some can attempt simple monoprints.

Year 1

The children should be encouraged to make their own blocks using different textures. Two colour prints can be achieved by using one colour on coloured paper. Children can continue exploring monoprints. Introduce the use of masking areas of ink.

Year 2

Children can experiment with stencil and template in preparation for screen printing. In addition to making their own blocks, children can be shown how to use material to make one colour 'press prints'.

Year 3

Children can be shown how to build up multiple colour prints - demonstrating relief and intaglio printing techniques. Children should be encouraged to work back into their prints with a variety of media. Continue exploring monoprints, use 'soft ground' technique.

Year 4

Children can use their own bodies to explore tessellation and overlapping. They can cut and reorganise finished prints and consider printing for a specific purpose.

Year 5

Children can combine their prints with other work to create mixed media work. Printing in other cultures and at other times may provide a starting point for children's own work. Children need to be involoved in selection and reflection and consider the exhibition of work.

Year 6

Children need to be provided with opportunities to demonstrate that they can make informed choices. They may be involved in creating group screen prints. Children will need to consolidate specific vocabulary and integrate it with general artistic knowledge and understanding.

Monoprinting

Each time a group of children engages in a printing activity, there is an opportunity, before the inking tray is washed, for some monoprinting. Essentially, a monoprint is a 'one-off' print. An inked surface can be 'drawn' into with fingers or found tools and then a sheet of paper laid across the surface to produce a print. The inked surface can also be masked with cut or torn paper. In addition, the surface can be lightly covered with a sheet of paper and this can be drawn on or pressed to transfer an image onto the paper. These techniques can be combined to produce a highly sophisticated image. Monoprinting could be explored progressively for its own sake.

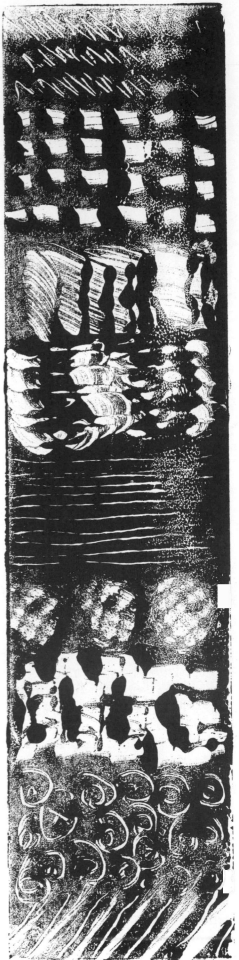

Extensions

There are enough activities and natural stages in printmaking to span the two key stages, progressively building upon skills and techniques as they are learned. Ideally, children will have had opportunities to use printmaking as a means of expression, printed for a variety of purposes and experimented with printing on a variety of surfaces including fabric.

When faced with a collection of multiple images, children may be encouraged to select a particularly successful print for display and consider some of the following for the other prints:

• Work back into the print with other mediums.

• Cut up and reorganise prints to provide new works or starting points.

• Scan pints into a computer and use software packages to further manipulate the images.

Looking at and discussing work by established printmakers will provide some initial starting points as well as informing the children about their own practise. Identifying work that has been generated as a result of the printmaking process rather than reproductions of drawn images, may be difficult at first, but the more their own practise and understanding develops, the easier they will find it. Illustrations in children's books are a useful starting point.

3D Work

Key Stage 1 and Key Stage 2 pupils can gain a wealth of experiences from working in 3D and should be given the opportunity to work with the different types of materials regularly. Each material will enable the pupils to explore a wide variety of experiences, both skills based and sensory. 3D work is the area that Ofsted feels is weak in most primary schools, yet when planned carefully can encompass many of the Programmes of Study in Design Technology as well as Art. The pupils should be given time to explore and experiment with the materials before skills are taught that will enable the pupils to use them correctly and then when confidence has been gained they can adapt, modify, change and invent to create high quality finished pieces of work.

Modelling

There are many kinds of modelling materials available and these include clay, dough, plasticine, Fimo, Soffmo etc.
Clay
There is no need for a kiln to produce high quality work when using clay. Some clays contain nylon fibres which make the air dry artefacts stronger, yet it is difficult to work with and reclaim. Buff clays and grey clays are easier to work with, will air dry and can be finished in a variety of ways. The pupils should be given a small piece of clay to work with at first so that it can be rolled, pulled, pushed and kneaded in an experimental way before a finished article is made.Key Stage 1 pupils can form a thumb pot from  a small ball of clay. To keep the clay moist over play-times, it should be covered with plastic or a damp paper towel or J cloth. Do not place a bowl of water on the table for pupils to use as they will use too much.   Provide damp sponges for the children to use to moisten their  fingers prior to smoothing the sides of the pots. Paper towel or a piece of hessian cloth should be placed under the clay to protect the surfaces and prevent the clay sticking to the tables. It also enables the children to write their names on the paper or cloth for identification purposes.When the pots have air dried they can be painted using ready mixed paints or powder paints and then varnished using P.V.A. and water in a 50 / 50 mix. Take care to dab on the varnish so that the painted decoration is not disturbed. The thumb pots can also be covered in shoe polish and then polished with a soft cloth to create a glazed effect. It is unwise to attempt with Key Stage 1 pupil's models with clay that have pieces attached as these often drop off during the drying. The pupils should be shown how animals and figures can be created by  pulling and working the clay in one piece and then they should be given time to experiment.Key Stage 2 pupils should be given time to explore the clay in structured skills activities so that they can pull, push, model and burrow into the clay using their fingers and pieces of equipment e.g. lolly sticks, plastic knives,

clay tools, nails etc. A simple coil pot can be created and decorated as before or the pupils can be taught how to roll out a piece of clay into a

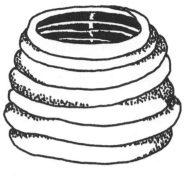

slab of even thickness to create a slab pot. To roll out the clay, use two pieces of strip wood as rolling guides and, placing the clay between the guides, use a rolling pin to roll out the clay forming an even slab. To remove the clay from the surface, use a piece of fishing line attached to

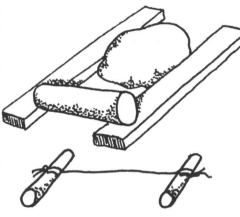

two pieces of dowel and pull it under the slab. From this slab of clay four sides can be cut to create a pot. The sides will need to be joined by using slip - a mixture of clay and water. Tiles can be made in this way, a square being cut from the slab and then decoration added by pushing tools or reclaimed objects into the clay to make impressions, indentations and decorations on the surface which can then be painted or

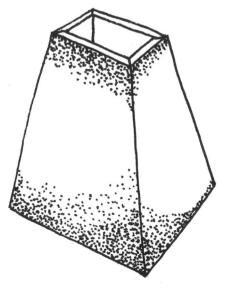

varnished. It is important that the clay the pupils are working with has been stored correctly in a plastic bag in an airtight bin. If the clay is to be reclaimed at the end of a session, it should be formed into a ball with a thumb hole pushed into it. The hole should then be filled with water, covered with clay and the clay placed into a polythene bag in the clay bin.

Plasticine

Most schools have plasticine and the benefits of pupils working with this material should not be underestimated. Make sure that the plasticine has not been stored for too long and that the essential oils are still present so that the plasticine does not crumble when it is worked with. It is a useful material for designing models and can be rolled, pulled and pushed into creating burrows and indents. Plasticine is a non permanent modelling material. However, its properties are very similar to a range of materials available that can be baked in an oven to become hard e.g. dough, Fimo, etc. These materials when baked can be varnished to become permanent artefacts as the baked materials cannot be reclaimed. The materials come in a wide variety of colours and are suitable for creating small pieces such as jewellery, beads and wall plaques.

Moulding Materials

Art Roc (Mod Roc)

This is a Plaster of Paris on a bandage and can be introduced to Key Stage 2 pupils.The bandage must be dipped into a bowl of water and although very wet at first, it dries quickly and can be smeered over any structure made of wire, withies, card, plastic and even ballons. When it is dry it can be painted with acrylic, ready

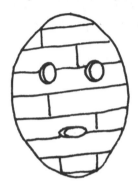 

mix or powder paints and P.V.A. or polyurethane varnish can be dabbed on to the decorated item. When working with Art Roc / Mod Roc certain precautions should be taken:

i) The material is messy to work with and tables / floors should be covered with plastic sheeting.

ii) Cut the bandage into small lengths before the process begins as large pieces when wet get easily tangled and scissors can get covered with the wet plaster.

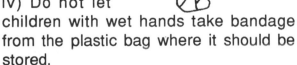

iii)Keep the dry pile of plaster bandage well away from the bowl of water.

iv) Do not let children with wet hands take bandage from the plastic bag where it should be stored.

v)The water container will have a residue of plaster at the bottom. This must be tipped onto newspaper and thrown away not disposed of down the sink as it will block the drain.

Papier Mache

Young children can cover a variety of objects in papier mache as it is easy to prepare and use and costs almost nothing to make. The children should first prepare the ripped newspaper squares or strips. The squares can be dipped into wallpaper paste (take care to buy wall paper paste that does not contain fungicide) whereas the strips should be coated with paste using a paint brush. Ball-oons are a favourite item for covering yet the outside of up-turned plastic bowls can be covered in plastic bags or cling film and covered with the papier mache. The items will need a long time to dry, up to a week depending on the layers of

newspaper used. When dry the pieces of work can be painted with ready mix paint, powder paint or chromacryl and varnished. Other collage materials can be glued onto the coloured pieces to enhance their finish.It is possible to purchase Art Mache, an instant papier mache which can be rolled or moulded and placed on plastic bottles to create spell bottles or paper plates to create faces and magic mirrors. The Art Mache is however difficult to handle and takes an extremely long time to dry.

Fabric and Wallpaper Paste

Fabrics can be soaked in wall paper paste and draped over frame and shell structures. This has the advantage that folds and draping effects can be created when the fabric is wet. When dry the fabric will be hard and the shape will be permanent. Decorated fabrics will not need painting although the children may wish to enhance the design with 3D paints.

Plastazote

Plastazote is an expanded polyethelene foam which can be heated for a very short time in a Baby Belling cooker and when it reaches its 'plastic' state it can be moulded over rigid shell structures and allowed to cool and it will retain the shape of the mould. It is very important that the manufacturers instructions are read fully before the material is worked with as there are hazards if it is misused. The plastazote comes in a variety of colours and is very effective as masks if moulded over polystyrene heads. An A4 sheet is suitable for a full face mask yet the pupils should be

given the choice between a full face mask, a three quarters and an eye mask. It would be advisable to make examples of these masks from plastazote to show the pupils prior to them designing their own and during the activity the adult will become more familiar with the material area and be aware of the problems that may arise.

Carving - A Reduction Process

Because of Health and Safety issues the tools used for carving must be carefully chosen to avoid accidents and the children should be given careful instructions as to the correct use of the tools to minimise risk. Plastic knives, lolly sticks, clay tools and surform blades can all be used to carve a variety of materials.

Clay

The clay should be shaped into a sphere, cone, cylinder or cuboid before carving takes place and then must be left for twenty four hours before it is needed. After this period the clay will have become 'leather hard' and can then be carved into simple shapes. Pebbles and bones can be carved from observation of actual items or abstract shapes can be experimented with. Look carefully at curves, sharp edges and angles in natural and man made objects and make observational drawings

which can be kept in a sketch book. Photographs and pictures from magazines can also be collected for ideas and reference. It is recommended that photographs are taken as a record of the activity during the exploration and experimental stages as well as photographs or drawings of the work produced. Some of the other materials suitable for carving have to be used with care.

Soap

Soap is suitable for carving yet the pupils must take care that the small pieces carved out do not get rubbed on their face as they would irritate if brought into contact with the eyes.

Plaster of Paris

The plaster of Paris should be made and set in individual polythene bags, yogurt pots or small boxes. (Make sure the seams are sealed with sticky tape.)

When the plaster has set the container should be removed and carving can take place. Take care - dust can be created and carving should take place only in a well ventilated area and the dust should be cleared away regularly.

Chalk

Blocks of chalk can be carved yet once again care must be taken as dust is created.

Construction

Pupils will need to be taught the correct use and type of equipment to use with the wide variety of materials used in a construction activity. The materials used are many and varied e.g. wire, card, reclaimed materials, artstraws, withies etc. and they will all need skills teaching lessons prior to the children using them to produce a finished article. It is essential that the children are shown how to correctly use the cutting equipment and this can include scissors, safety and utility snips, hole punches, craft knives, cutting mats and safety rulers.

Scissors

Key Stage 1 pupils should be provided with left and right handed round ended scissors that cut! So often the scissors that pupils are given to use are of poor quality and the children become frustrated because of inferior equipment which is beyond their control. The adults working with the children should have pointed ended scissors to show pupils how to cut holes from the centre of pieces of paper or card and this

technique should only be demonstrated to young children. Key Stage 2 pupils should be provided with a variety of scissors, small and large, with round and pointed ends to enable them to make the correct choices and select the most appropriate scissors for a specific task.

Utility Snips and Safety Snips

When Key Stage 1 pupils are involved in construction using reclaimed materials they should be introduced to utility snips which work in the same way as scissors yet are more appropriate for cutting through thick card and plastic bottles.

On reaching Key Stage 2 pupils can be shown the correct way to use safety snips which work on the principal of secateurs having a spring mechanism. These are slightly more dificult to use than utility snips although perform the same task and they rquire a larger hand to grasp the handles and apply pressure to operatethe plier action. At Key Stage 2 both utility snips and safety snips should be available to enable the pupils to make a choice according to their personal preferences.

Hole Punches

Pieces of equipment to make holes in card and paper come in a variety of shapes and sizes. Single hole punches can be used to make decorations around the edge of a paper plate to thread ribbon through or they can be used to create holes through which brass fasteners, star binders or eyelets can be attached creating a joining that allows movement. Double and four hole puches can also be experimented with to

ensure accurate positioning. It is now possible to purchase hole punches that create decorative holes in a variety of shapes and sizes e.g. stars, snowflakes, trees, bears etc. The children should experiment with papers of different textures and thicknesses to see how easy the piece of equipment is to use and how accurately the holes can be positioned.

Paper Drills

Paper drills are very easy to use and come with nozzles of various sizes to cut holes. They have the advantage that they can cut out holes in the centre of large pieces of materials unlike the other hole punches that can only cut holes near the edge of the paper or card.

Craft Knives

Only retractable knives should be in primary schools and they should only ever be used under close supervision in conjunction with a cutting mat and safety ruler as they are all sharp enough to cut flesh. Children must be shown the correct way to use these pieces of equipment and then they should be given time to practice the skills taught. The practice examples can be kept in the children's sketchbooks to be used for reference purposes and notes should be made as to the use and effect of the equipment.

Shell Structures

Within the area of construction materials, some are suitable for creating shell structures, others are sutable for frame structures.

Paper and Card

Key Stage 1 pupils should be taught how to fold different kinds of paper and card e.g. tissue paper, sugar paper, thick card, 4 sheet thickness card, wrapping paper, cartridge paper etc. in different ways e.g. in half, thirds, quarters, concertina folds etc. Key Stage 2 pupils can fold card in a variety of ways to create 3D models and measuring can be incorporated in the tasks to ensure accuracy. Cutting skills should be practiced in a structured series of activities to develop co-ordination skills and a quality finish.

Key Stage 1 pupils should:

1) Cut along straight, curved and zig zag lines.

2) Cut out simple 2D shapes.

3) Cut out more complex 2D shapes.

4) Be introduced to the four basic pop up cuts.

5) Be taught how to cut a hole from the centre of a mount.

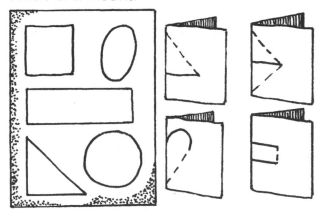

Key Stage 2 pupils should:

1) Cut accurately along pre drawn lines.

2) Cut out complex 2D shapesaccurately.

3) Be introduced to Key Stage 2 developments of Key Stage 1 cuts to create pop up cards and dioramas.

4) Be taught how to join card and paper using cut tabs and slots. (All of these

techniques are detailed in 'Pop-Up Cards' published by Topical Resources.)

Curling and Bending

Curling and bending techniques can be taught to Key Stage 1 children and practised so that in Key Stage 2 they can apply the knowledge to their own designs. Key Stage 1 pupils should be

shown how to disassemble cardboard boxes and remake them inside out to create a clean surface onto which decoration can be added and time should be allowed for the rearranging of components during an activity.

Joining Techniques

Joining techniques should be experimented with in Key Stage 1 so that

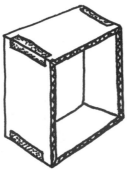

in Key Stage 2 the children select the most appropriate technique and equipment e.g. brown tape, double sided tape, sticky tape, P.V.A. glue, low melt glue gun, paper fasteners, staples, paper clips, brass fasteners, star binders, string etc. Skills can be introduced to Key Stage 1 and Key Stage 2 pupils through focussed tasks when they can create greetings cards, gift boxes, packaging, paper bag puppets and paper and card sculptures representing creatures, fruit segments etc. Finishing skills should

also be explored. Key Stage 1 pupils will need adult guidance and once the colourings and collage materials have been used under supervision, Key Stage 2 pupils can be given a range of materials from which they can select the most suitable e.g. chromacryl paints, 3D paints, felt pens, beads, sequins, pom poms, coverings etc..

Reclaimed Materials (Junk Modelling)

Cutting, folding, slotting, joining and finishing skills can be transferred from paper and card experiences to activities using reclaimed materials e.g. cardboard boxes, plastic bottles, card cylinders, yogurt pots etc. Finishing and joining techniques must be explored and experimented with extensively during Key Stage 1 to prepare the children for activities during Key Stage 2 where the application of skills taught will be assessed. Utility and Safety snips are essential pieces of equipment for cutting and shaping card and plastic and a low melt glue gun is recommended for neat and permanent joinings of plastic to plastic and plastic to card. Cardboard tubes can be joined to flat surfaces using tabs and these are made by cutting slots downwards around the edge of the tube and folding them outwards creating tabs which can be glued securing the cylinder securely to the surface. If a cardboard

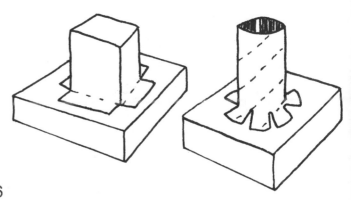

tube is drawn around onto a box then a hole can be cut out the same diameter as the tube and the cylinder placed into the hole, pushed to the base of the box and secured around the hole with glue of brown sticky tape creating a rigid structure. Jewellery can be created from reclaimed materials yet care must be taken to distinguish

between a prototype and actual jewellery. Prototypes, the designs, can be made from card tubes, rolled newspaper and plastic pieces to experiment with shape and size whereas when the design is made into the actual jewellery, decoration and size is important to create a functional piece of body adornment which can be worn. A varied collection of reclaimed materials should be made available to the pupils e.g. brass hinges, buttons, clay beads, artstraws, lolly sticks, paper beads, plastic tubing, paper clips, plastic bottles and plastic pots etc.

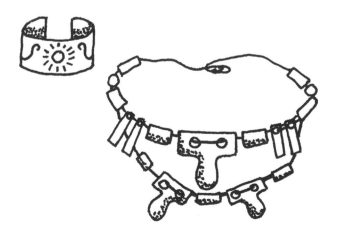

Frame Structures

Wire, artstraws, wood, rolled newspaper and withies can all be used to create frameworks but some of the materials are not suitable for Key Stage 1 pupils.

Wire

A Key Stage 2 material which must be used with care because of the sharp ends and protective gloves can be worn to protect the pupils hands. Wire cutters and pliers should be used to cut, shape and twist the wire to create for example figures and animals. The wire is used to 'draw' in 3D and finished objects do not need to be covered as the lines suggest movement. It enhances the

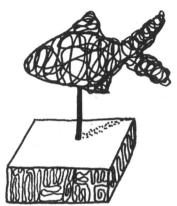

finished model to display it appropriately and this can include a wooden base with a hole drilled the centre into which the support wire is glued.

Withies
(Willow Bundles)

The traditional basket makers raw material suitable for KS2. Useful for constructing large scale models e.g. insects, birds, animals, environments, kites etc. They are very springy and need soaking in water for about twenty

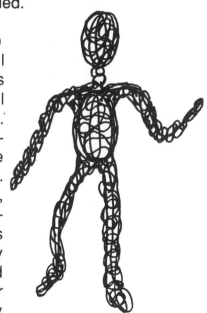

minutes prior to use and this can be done in a large sink or a piece of drainpipe with a stopper on the end is ideal. After soaking the withies are able to be curved, twisted and shaped and can be cut with the utility or safety snips and joined with masking tape, wire or string. When the structure is completed it can stand alone or be woven into, tied onto or covered with for example tissue paper or newspaper covered in P.V.A., papier mache, Mod Roc. or fabric soaked in wall paper paste.

ArtStraws

Artstraws can be used by Key Stage 1 and Key Stage 2 pupils as they are economical, easy to cut, bend, join and colour. They can be used to create a variety of frame structures and can be incorporated into jewellery. Towers can be made by joining artstraw sections with pipe cleaners which will enable corners to be created and tall stable

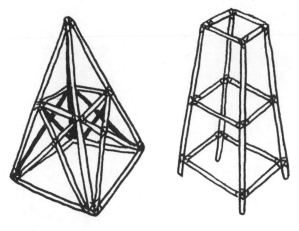

Newspaper

Sheets of newspaper can be rolled diagonally and then twisted and plaited to create a framework. The strips can be joined with masking tape.

Wood

Strip wood and square section wood can be used to create frame structures when used with triangulated corner strengtheners. To cut the wood accurately the Key Stage 2 pupils should be taught how to use a junior hacksaw and a bench hook and the technique should be taught in a focussed way constructing for example a cuboid which can then be clad in card to create a gift box or building. (For detailed instructions on the uses of triangulated corner strengtheners read "Moving Toys and Models" published by Topical Resources.)

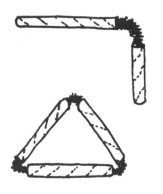

structures can be achieved. Weaving with artstraws through card or notched weaving looms results in a textured effect which can be made more interesting if the artstraws are coloured or decorated prior to the weaving activity. Artstraws can also be glued onto or attached with sticky tape onto a card band and this can be made into a hat band. The tops of the straws can be gathered with tape and the hat woven through or covered with tissue paper.

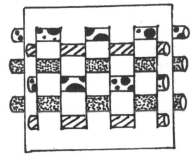

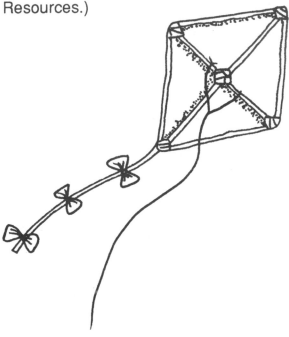

Sketchbooks

What are sketchbooks?

Sketchbooks are better called an "Art Ideas Book". They are a place for ideas for art rather like an English draft book is a place for ideas for stories and other writing.

They form a visual record of the artists studied, techniques and media experienced as well as evidence of developing skills in observation and design.

They are the place where the 'arts' can come together with music, poetry and art complimenting each other.

How do I begin?

First you will need suitable materials for a sketchbook. This can range in quality and price from a spiral bound sketchbook to pieces of paper stapled together to form a book. Go for the best quality paper that you can afford, but don't let a tight budget put you off!

Blank pages, especially the first page of a new sketchbook, are always off putting. "What if I make a mess and ruin the whole thing?" This can be over come by breaking up the surface. Stick related text and pictures alongside roughly sketched boxes.e.g.

eyelashes *eyebrows* EYES
pupils **IRIS** tearduct

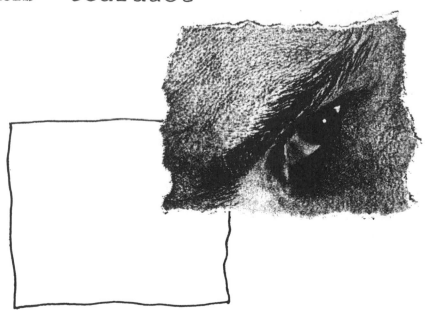

Begin by making quick sketches and observations of parts of the subject. This is more likely to give better results rather than attempting the whole thing straight away.

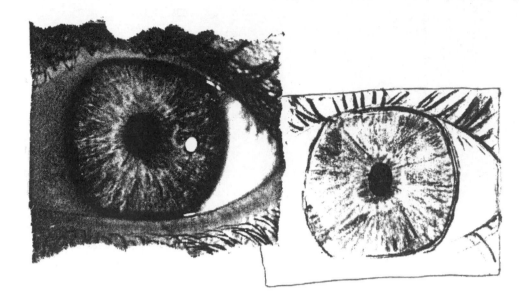

Use torn edges rather than cut to create an exciting and lively feel.

Combine images, text and colour for interesting effects.

It is good idea to prepare a sheet of related images and words for use in the sketchbook. Collect newspapers, magazines etc. Tear out pictures and 'type associated words' in a varity of fonts and sizes. Older children could do this themselves given a wide range of materials and access to a word processor. These sheets could then be photocopied or several could be made up.

Perhaps the best way to understand the sketchbook is to see an example. This is part of a sketchbook for a Year 2 child called Rachel. The topic is 'Portraits'. This format could be copied exactly or adapted to suit other topics.

Page 1

On Rachel's first page she has close up pictures of eyes and an ear, as well as associated words in a variety of fonts. These were prepared by the teacher but older children could make their own. She sketched boxes alongside the pictures and used them for observational drawing. She also made quick notes at the side to remind her of the media she had used. Younger children may need help with what to write but older ones should be able to write unaided.

Further down the page she has eyes drawn from direct observation making colour studies at the side and comments at the bottom about how pleased she was with the colours. She wrote a poem about eyes which she typed up and stuck in near the drawings.

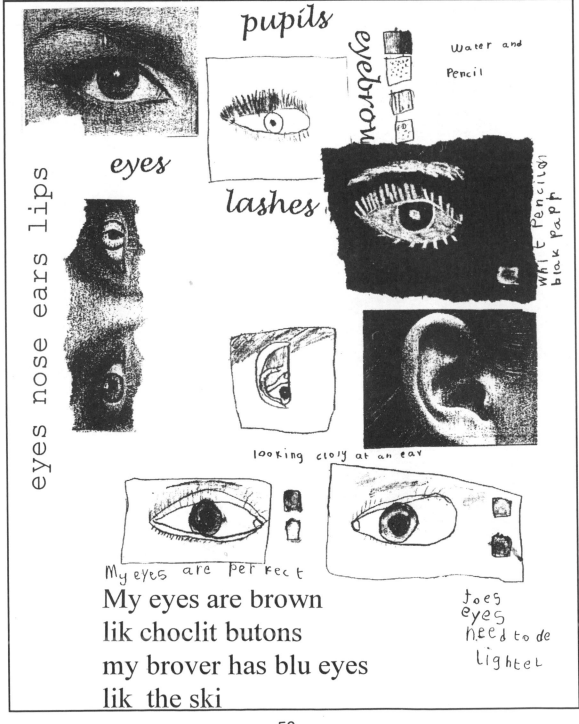

52

Page 2

Now Rachel begins to move away from small scale studies and attemts to draw a full face, one from observation, the other from memory. The close up studies she did for eyes are reflected in the detail included in the full face. She also uses techniques and media which she tried out on the previous page with developing skill and control.

Again she puts in a piece of poetry, and associated words. She still likes to use boxes to confine her work.

faces faces faces faces

brown
green
blue

blue eyes

drawing of a Face

My mums face is very nice
she smiles with her teth
and her eyes

a drawing of my mum with pencil and water

this is good for skin

I did the hair with pencil and water

Page 3

Rachel continues to make careful observations, extending her range of media to include pastel, paint and print.

The use of torn edges adds vitality and interest to the work.

faces faces faces faces faces

WATER cRayons on grey papr

I brew a mans fase
I copleb it out of the newspapr

Oil pastel ON blak papr

Page 4

Rachel begins to move away from representational work, although there is still some direct observation. She makes a collage of the man's face and takes rubbings. She continues to make notes on how she did things and things she has learned, for example, "If you are doing the hair you have got to wash the brush before you do the skin."

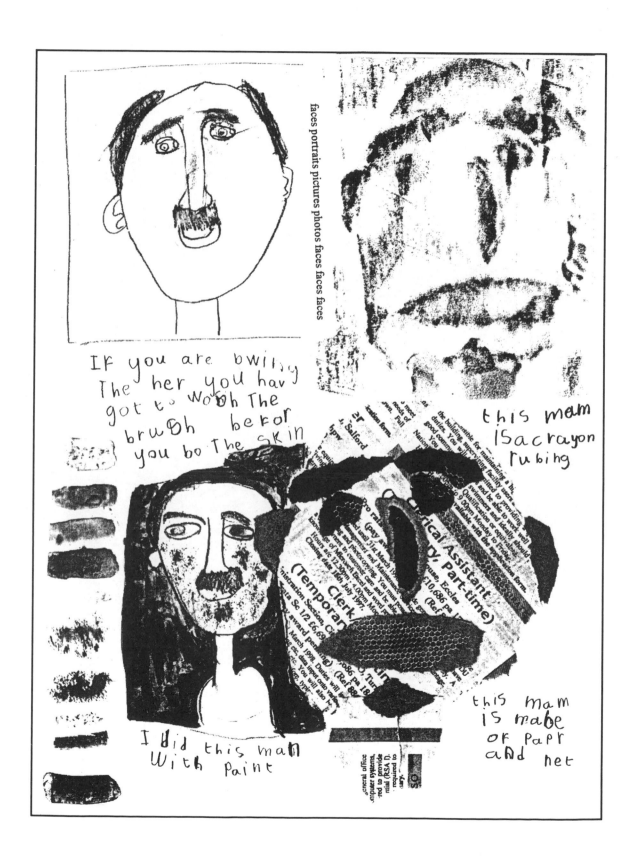

faces portraits pictures photos faces faces faces

IF you are bwihg The her you hav got to wolBh The bruBh beror you bo The skin

this mam isacrayon rubing

I Bid this mah With paint

this mam is mabe oF paPr aHd net

Page 5

Rachel is introduced to other artists work and she makes small samples in the style of the artist to see whether she likes the effect. She also adds some text about the artists which was prepared by the teacher. Older children could research their own. She adds her impressions and thoughts.

David Hockney is English, he was born in 1937. He used his camera to record his travels, friends and family. Hockney made a photomontage of his Mother in 1985. He took several shots, cut them up and pasted them back together to give a complete portrait.

We haveed look at David Hockney

I have brawll grandma I cut it up like David Hockney

I liked the Picher by David Hakney becose it look nise with gaps in it

faces faces faces faces faces faces faces

Page 6

Rachel continues to consider other artists work. She tries out their ideas and begins to make them her own, combining different aspects. Her design work is evolving and she is beginning to consider what she might like to do as a finished piece. The influences of the other artists is clear, but the work is made her own by using the ideas; rather than copying them.

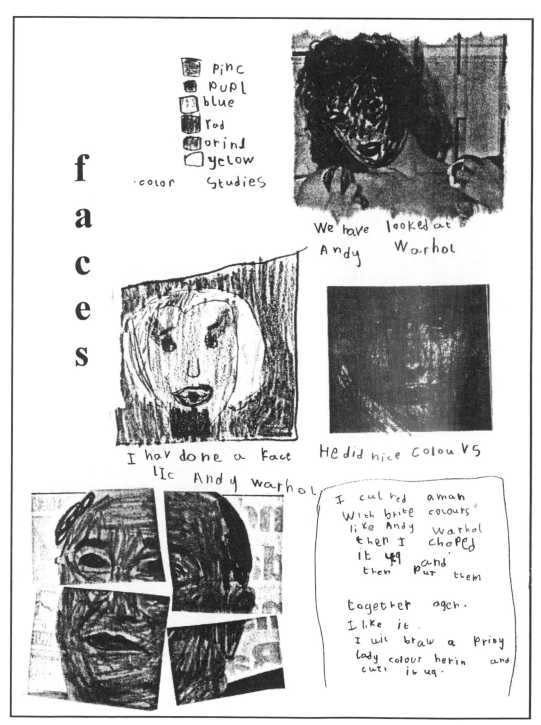

This brief introduction to sketchbooks has given you a model to copy or adapt for use in the classroom. It is a good idea to share sketchbooks within the class and with older children. Share wih partners or in small groups to encourage discussion of techniques, media and ideas.

Don't be afraid. Try out new ideas. There are no hard and fast rules about what should go into a sketchbook.
GOOD LUCK!

Display

The majority of teachers agree that the quality of the environment of a school can have a positive effect on the pupils. When children have produced work, mounting an effective display (be it about maths, science, history etc.) can be daunting and time consuming. This section aims to offer hints and advice to help the busy classroom teacher to avoid pitfalls and to make the most effective use of time and materials available.

Display should aim to encourage children to :

• observe their environment both inside and outside school.

• to question what? why? how? where? and when?

• to investigate using different art materials plus quizzes, games, research, questionnaires etc. and social interaction in making and using role play areas.

Types of Display

Displays fall into four categories and during the school year all will have their parts to play in contributing to children's learning.

Stimulus Display - designed to arouse interest, and focus attention on a particular concept or theme (often the type of display that starts a new term).

Informative Display - designed to introduce knowledge or provide summaries / reference related to projects etc. Information boards for parents / visitors about extra curricular events and clubs would be included in this category.

Interactive Display - designed to invite involvement, touching, looking, describing - this will include questions, opportunities to respond and collaborative collections on a theme.

Celebratory Displays - designed to show finished work and pride in achievement to a wider audience.

Displays should aim to be eye catching and pleasing, simple rather than complicated and respect and enhance the content. Where and how to begin? - read on.

The preparation of good displays will take considerable time and effort but the educational pay off can be enormous.

Points to Consider

• Plan the layout.

• Aim for simplicity not overcrowding.

• Colour co-ordination - personal preference will intervene here.

• Continuity throughout the room and adjoining area - purple boards next to orange boards do not harmonise!

• Clear lettering and labels - unify by colour or by choosing mounting paper from the same colour family.

• Progression of work i.e. include skill

building exercise that show the development of a theme.

•Stimulus material alongside the childreník work

• Reading matter / questions displayed at the children's eye level where possible.

• Each individual child should have work on display at some time.

• Regular spaces between pieces of work

• Tidy or cover adjacent areas - or they will distract.

• Check that your staple gun is loaded and that you have a good supply of spare staples!

Points to Avoid

• Cutting irregular bubbles around children's work.

• Using pinking shears.

• Using drawing pins. - except on staff and parent notice boards.

 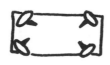

• Mounting pictures on a slant.

• Garish colour combinations - keep fluorescent paper to a minimum, if at all!

• Fussy, unnecessary drapes and borders.

• Single mounts that are too thin - and lack strength.

• Lack of contrast between mounting and backing papers allowing them to 'blend in' ineffectively.

• Too many black boards - black is safe but too much and school becomes funeral.

A Display Kit

• Staple gun and staples - an all metal gun works best and survives longest!

• Paper trimmer.

• Blu -Tack.

• Ruler.

• Copydex.

• Hand 'Bambi' stapler and staples.

• Staple extractor.

• Scissors large and small.

• Letter templates.

• Black felt pens, thick and thin.

• Pin push and straight pins.

• Metallic pencils.

• Ball of cotton.

• Strips of card of different lengths and widths.

Also make your own 'display' book that has a collection of the display papers available in school - examples of successful colour combinations - photographs of previous displays plus displays in colour magazines. This resource will help decision making easier.

Backing the Board

Colour choice will always reflect personality. We all have colours we prefer and will choose to use and others we will choose to avoid. In choosing a background paper remember it needs to work effectively with the paper on which the work is mounted - avoid too much contrast and similarly too little. Look for colour clues in the children's work if it is art related.

If in doubt -

• Orange, gold, brown, are rich.

• Natural / earth colours (brown, green etc.) fade very little and are sympathetic, particularly to observational work.

• Red and yellow glow to create an exciting display area.

• Green, blue, and white are fresh and crisp.

• Red, green and white contrast successfully.

Try also to work around existing room colours e.g. walls, doors, trays, curtains, particularly if the work is non art in content and offers less colour clues.

Sheets of paper can prove easier to handle than rolls particularly if there is a light switch or part of an alarm system to cut around. If boards are long and thin, continuing the backing paper above the board will enlarge the display area.

If the display board is soft the staples will go in easily - but will not be so easy to get out! To avoid this, stick a piece of card on the base of the staple gun. This will push the gun slightly away from the board and the staples, whilst attaching the work, will leave a slightly protruding lip for easy extraction.

Mounting Work

 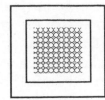

Single Mounting - quick and effective. A single black line drawn around the picture a little way from the edge can lead the eye in and give the impression of a double mount.

Double Mounting - use a variety of mount sizes to frame pictures - broad on narrow and vice versa rather then two identical widths. A small image looks more effective on a large mount.

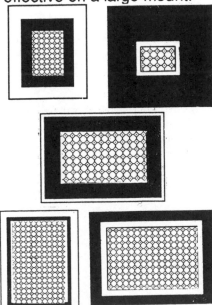

Triple Mounting - this extends the amount of frame further and involves a rather lavish use of materials.

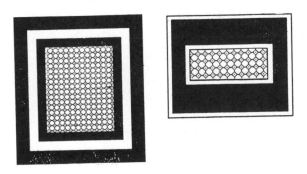

Before you start make sure that all work is trimmed and mounted square.

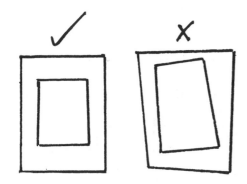

If gluing pictures to mounts remember that some adhesives crinkle paper. Stapling is more economical than gluing, allowing mounts to be used again. Use small staples and keep them in line with the work.

Make sure that children have ownership of their work and that their names are on either the work or the mount.

Metallic pencils work well on dark mounts. The use of the computer for labels and names is an effective use of IT that can involve the children themselves.

Arranging the Display

Most display boards are square or rectangular in shape and it is important to consider this when planning the layout of a display. Displays are more effective if the work runs parallel to the edges of the board leaving a border around the outside.

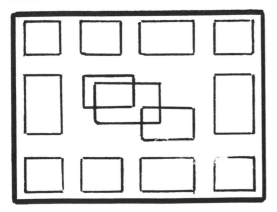

If work is to overlap and cluster this will be better in the centre of such an arrangement again leaving a border.

Regular Arrangements

In regular arrangements papers must be cut to the same size. Aim for a balanced arrangement with even and fairly close spacing. Too much space between pieces of work creates an empty floating feeling. A strip of card cut to the width of the agreed space and held between the work will keep the spaces regular.

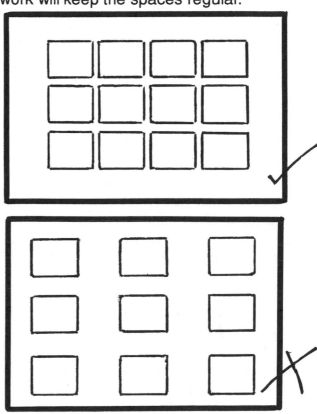

Hanging on a Line

Keep the tops of the work level - or the bottoms if hanging upwards. Pin a length of string in a straight line for the work to follow.

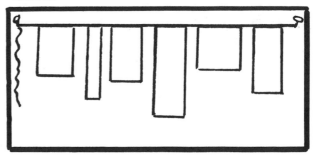

The string can be readily removed when the display is complete having ensured that the line is straight throughout the display and not almost straight!

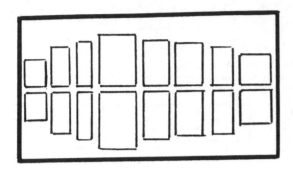

Alternatively a double line can be arranged above and below a central line - as in a reflection.

Irregular Arrangements

Arrangements of pieces of work which are of different shapes and sizes - irregular - present certain problems. It

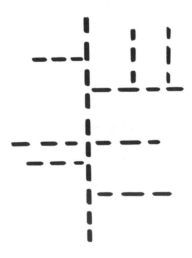

might be useful in this case to consider the display surface as a grid of strong vertical and horizontal 'lines of balance' that provide a framework on which the work can hang. They will give the display order and stability. To unify the arrangement the work must be fitted closely together in a cluster keeping the spaces even. Arrange the strongest shapes to the centre and place the smaller pieces further out. Try not to overcrowd the board and leave a breathing space all around the edge.

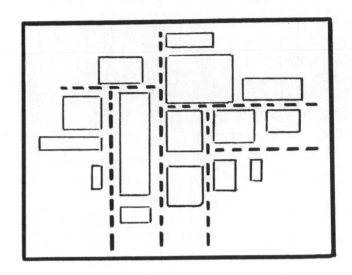

Working on a Cross

When displaying on a square board a strong vertical and horizontal cross can be established on which to arrange pieces of work.

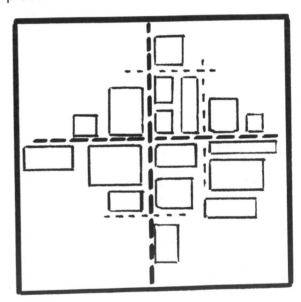

Keep the spacing even and again arrange larger pieces to the centre and smaller pieces towards the edges. Always work from the centre outwards. Line up tops or bottoms of work where possible.

Unmounted Work

Work can look attractive unmounted if it is clustered together in a group to unify it and the spacing between the pieces is even.

Take care to ensure a good contrast of colour between the work and the background. Light on dark or dark on light will have maximum impact.

If in doubt about an arrangement - set out the display on the floor space below the board to see how it will fit together - before you commit yourself.

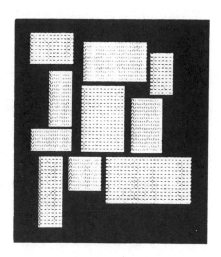

Borders

Many commercially produced borders are now available. They offer a range of colours, shapes, textures and themed illustrations that can add to a display. Remember the purpose of the border is to enhance and unite the display not to detract. Borders can be used effectively to divide up large boards, to tidy edges of unsightly boards or introduce colour and interest to a board display. Caution at all times or the display can become too fussy and lose impact.

Lettering

Try using - stencils, overhead projectors, photocopiers, letter templates, computers, commercial lettering.

Aim for - readability, simple captions / questions, even lettering, lettering in proportion to the board.

Attractive displays can be spoilt by poorly produced labels and lettering. Consider the position of the lettering for easy reading. Ensure that the lettering blends in with the display but is not 'lost'. Keep writing to a minimum for maximum impact. Ensure that the labels on displays are smaller in size than the title so that they do not vie for attention. Letter templates and computer lettering will help raise the standard of lettering in displays and also give a degree of uniformity to headings and captions. Cut out letters can help to carry colour through a display if the letters are matched to the mounting paper used. Cut letters from magazine pictures or wrapping paper related to the subject or from experimental sheets of e.g. marbling or printing. Two letters cut from contrasting colours and slightly offset acquire a certain depth and 3D quality. Enlarge and reduce lettering using a photocopier. Use work on display to underline a title or group the display around the title as a focus.

3D Display

Some work for display will be three dimensional and cannot be pinned to the wall. Children's models and stimulus material eg. a collection

of shells present problems particularly when space is limited. Different levels need to be created and a lot can be done using e.g. stage blocks, tins, boxes, bricks, flower pots etc.

When setting out the display group and sequence objects to guide the eye across the display. Consider the scale of the work

from the front to back so that the objects are not obscured. If you want to emphasize a particular item stand it on its own. Light 3D models or clay tiles that have the necessary hanging hole made in them can be suspended from a board using a pin push and straight dressmaker pins.

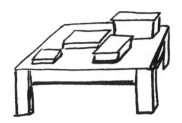

Windows

These may be a large percentage of the display area in a new building. Painted windows can contribute greatly to a theme e.g. 'Underwate'r. Make sure the paint used is designed for this purpose so that it will resist condensation, not block out the light or flake off.

Storage

This too will contribute to display in the classroom. Colour co-ordinate storage boxes and trays. A set of identical tins, boxes or jars labelled clearly and uniformly is more pleasing than the visual chaos of unrelated containers.

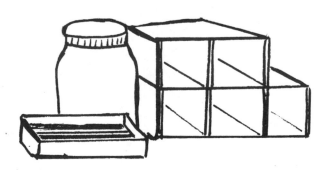

The School Environment

Each area of the school presents a different challenge when it comes to display.
The classroom - This is the working area and should reflect current work. Finished and unfinished work should be on show to indicate how work is progressing. The aim is to provide a stimulating environment.

Corridors and Central Areas - Displays in these areas can be more static. It is in these areas that children have the opportunity to see the work of other children of different ages. Work can be circulated from classroom to corridor to share topic and themes and celebrate achievement. Interactive questions are needed to invite the viewer to find out more about the displays and their content.

The Entrance or Hall Area - This is an area of scene setting and gives messages about the school to visitors. Here the quality of display needs to reach a high standard to show the work off at its best. It should be the work from any / all age groups and not concentrate on the best work of year 6 only! This area should confront the visitor with honest and excellent achievement which will encourage the visitor / viewer to see the work displayed in the rest of the school in the right context.

From the earliest age children should be engaged with the display of their work - deciding on work to be displayed, where it should go etc. until eventually (with practice!) it should be possible for children to mount and display exhibitions of their own.

Finally any display should succeed through the quality of the children's work. Good display will enhance it - bad sloppy display can do the reverse. Good display draws attention.

So remember keep it simple, beware of overkill and then celebrate your own part in successfully displaying children's work in school.